PUBLIC SPIRIT

AND

MOBS.

TWO SERMONS DELIVERED AT SPRINGFIELD, MASS., ON SUNDAY, FEBRUARY 23, 1851, AFTER THE THOMPSON RIOT.

BY

GEORGE F. SIMMONS,
PASTOR OF THE THIRD CONGREGATIONAL SOCIETY.

SPRINGFIELD:
MERRIAM, CHAPIN, & CO.
BOSTON:
WM. CROSBY AND H. P. NICHOLS.
1851.

There are some words in these discourses which I would change or omit; but to guard against misconstruction, I have, on the advice of friends, had them printed verbally, without alteration, inserting, in one place, some explanatory words in parenthesis.— They are very poor attempts in a very great cause.

CAMBRIDGE:
METCALF AND COMPANY,
PRINTERS TO THE UNIVERSITY.

SERMON I.

PUBLIC SPIRIT.

AND WHEN HE WAS COME NEAR, HE BEHELD THE CITY, AND WEPT OVER IT, SAYING, IF THOU HADST KNOWN, EVEN THOU, AT LEAST IN THIS THY DAY, THE THINGS WHICH BELONG UNTO THY PEACE! BUT NOW THEY ARE HID FROM THINE EYES. — Luke xix. 41, 42.

I INTENDED this morning to preach with reference to the late disturbances among us; but finding that there had unavoidably entered into my discourse much that was civic and municipal, and that it was a very painful and troublesome subject, I concluded to defer it to the afternoon, and to prepare our minds for that duty by something in which we could have greater religious enjoyment and repose. I propose therefore to you the text, on which I shall first have something to say of the person, of his act, and of the reason for it.

Who is it that breaks out into this flood of tears, as, arriving at the summit of the Mount of

Olives, he looks down on the doomed city of Jerusalem? It is Jesus Christ, the man of Nazareth, the healer of the sick, the teacher of truth, the soon-to-be-crucified, the Saviour of the world, whom nations now honor, and not a few obey;—a man whom we conceive in the dignity of a great office, with the serenity of heaven on his face and the tranquillity of God in his demeanor, the Wonderful, the Counsellor, the Prince of Peace. He had labored for the people's good, and sought it with a single aim. He had declared the truth of God which alone could save it, and he was prepared to offer up himself in its behalf. The Almighty Father was in him, in his heart; he lived consciously in the surrounding presence of the Father; those counsels which decreed the salvation of the world in him, were open to his mind as the day; and yet there was that patriot feeling in his heart which could not be removed by considerations of the world's advantage, but when he saw the holy city on the ruins of which his salvation was to triumph,—the city of David, which a series of prophets had loved even while it abused them,—when he looked upon those towers which were to be laid low, and that deluded population which thronged, with inward and with outward steps, the gates, to which his unheeded word of tenderness had been so often spoken,—the channels of grief were broken up, and tears of human sympathy streamed from those overladen eyes, in which divine serenity was wont habitually to repose. His weeping was not the weeping of a sentimentalist, nor the weeping of a sinner. It was the weeping of a teacher, and a patriot, at the prospective woes of a community of which he formed a living part, and whose disease he could no longer hope to heal.

If his grief had been over a losing side, with which he had been defeated, — if it had been grief that he was not honored, or contrition that he had not done his part, — if it had been, finally, sensibility at having been insulted, and terror at being about to be executed, — it might have been touching, but it would not have had the character it has. For this was not a personal, but a common sorrow, and though his own blood was soon to seal his prophecy, he was now moved by the general woe, and not by his own.

What, then, more specifically was the subject of the Saviour's tears?

It was that the city he loved was going to ruin, through intestine disorders, in consequence of the immoralities of the people, and for want in them of that faith of God which gives strength to every community, as it gives dignity to every individual.

For you are all aware of the intimate connection there was between the unruly obstinacy of inhabitants of Jerusalem, — which, having its root in a perverse faith and fanatical theories of society, broke out in perpetual excesses, — and the destruction of the city by a Roman army. It was only an instance of those frequent retributions which, though naturally resulting from actions, fall upon people wholly unawares to them, because they are lost in dreams of different consequences of their conduct from what infinite justice ordains. The Jewish Sicarii had a righteousness of their own. The assassins had a code of laws, and prescribed measures to the citizens.

The guidance of the people was given up to that class of men called in the Old Testament "the sons of Belial"; and the consequence was this memorable one, not that enemies subdued the brave and resisting city, but that they devoured themselves, and exhibited within the walls first a hell upon earth, before the towers were laid low, and "the abomination of desolation" possessed the place, and scattered the small remnant of the people to the four winds of heaven, to be thenceforth, as dwellers in strange cities, as outcasts and wanderers on the earth, monuments of the Divine vengeance to all the inhabitants of the world for ever.

But this is but a picture in large of what is often transpiring. It is a great church picture of what we have among ourselves in miniature. But men who are blind can no more see themselves in a mirror, than they can see the path of justice and safety to walk in. A man blind to the truth is blind also to himself. This is a universal rule.

The real cause of the ruin of the Jews was, that they lost their religion. They had no longer that practical guide of life, that *supreme* guide of life. And consequently the popular character became degraded, violent, and headstrong; and not justice, but will, was the rule of civil action. Jesus Christ saw this, not merely in its results, but in its sources; and it was at the sources that he labored to correct the popular heart. Men sometimes suppose that that which concerns people's faith is not practical. But it is more profoundly practical than all things else, inasmuch as the whole of life flows out of it. The

Jewish people was diseased in its faith, in its religious character. That was the fatal fountain of all and of infinite evil. And hence Jesus labored to restore to them what they had lost, to quicken by a new and fresh belief in God all the generous instincts of the soul, and to form characters which should endure the trials of terrible times. And now, having labored in vain, having reclaimed only a few individuals out of a multitude of the guilty, a few atoms out of the sea of perdition, — having proved that it was useless for the daughter of Zion that he should live, he prepared, for it and for all mankind, to die; and looking upon the city in this temper and with this despair, he wept over it, and exclaimed, "O that thou hadst known, even in this thy day, the things that belong to thy peace! *But they are hid from thine eyes.*" This is Jesus the Saviour of the world. It is Jesus the Son of God, anointed with great spiritual power. But it is also the citizen of Nazareth, the lover of his Hebrew fathers' land. And it is no disgrace to religion to unite with it the love of one's residence, and to blend the patriot and the Christian all in one.

Yet it is an instance of how personal and public feeling may coincide in a just man's heart, that the greatest curse to fall on that city over which he mourned was his own death, their rejection and murder of the Son of God. If his heart, then, was resting on that crucifixion, it was not a merely individual suffering; for the Son of God was excluded from their souls when the Son of Man was slaughtered. The hope of their nation died with him. He was so perfectly identified with the true good of Zion, that with him it ended for ever; and so his cause of tears, so far as it naturally may have had mingled in it reference to his crucifixion, included in it extinction of hope of a revived faith in Israel. Until his death, Jesus lived for his own country. But after he had risen, his country had no more share in him. He was then the Saviour of the world. The opportunity for conversion to the Jews was passed. The doom had been written in the book of God, that mankind was to advance over the dead body of the daughter of Zion; and only a few exiles of her children enjoy the brightness of the coming day. So the day was now approaching, when the heart of Jesus was to be separated from his race for ever. The tender bond was softly broken, and his love went out in tears. We see the citizen gradually expiring within him; and from his pains and mortifications and lamentations there rose the citizen of the universe. This inward death and resurrection was in truth completed only in the last sacrifice, was simultaneous, therefore, with the death and resurrection of his body. And I may add, that, by a faint resemblance, it is through a similar pain that every man passes who survives his pride in the land of his birth. Love of country is a strong and universal instinct; and it is carried by most generous natures, in spite of other principles that contend with it, to the dying hour. But it is ever to be held in subjection to moral truth, and should not blind the mind to the will of God, and to those ties which connect people of all nations of the earth.

II. From this scene of Christ's weeping on the Mount of Olives, I would deduce the reflection, that, in order, so to speak, to earn the right of mourning the lapses of the community, we must first, as he did, labor for its good. We ought to feel bound to labor for the country, in the way of raising its character and purifying its manners. That is a great cause, in which we all, as citizens, are banded together. The character of the community is our common fund. Its reputation is our common pride. Its hopes are common to us all. And we and our children share in the soul which belongs to the mass. We are, as it were, members of one body, limbs, far more than we imagine, of a living organism. And this is proved by the tears with which a person of heavenly connections, like Jesus, broke the ties by which his heart was bound to his people. So we cannot separate ourselves. Henceforth unto death we are members of a living society; and all *its* interests are *ours*. And in the particular country in which our lot is cast, we are to labor, as for life, for the improvement of character, for the melioration of manners, and for bettering the condition of the people. This is the great object in pursuit of which all are one, and on which all depends. The public peace, the public morals, the public manners, the public government, the public instruction, — those great concerns of every one should be the diligent study of the good. So it was with Jesus. These were his earnest aim and loving endeavor, his sole work, so far as he was limited to Israel. And he only extended the same spirit when he disseminated his religion abroad. So he cried, "Woe unto thee, Capernaum!" and "Woe unto thee, Bethsaida!" with the sad tone of an injured and forsaken friend, as the virtuous bridegroom would lament for his wandered bride, — and "O Jerusalem! Jerusalem! thou that stonest the prophets," as if the spirit which had guided the nation was singing its dirge over the falling city.

2. But another lesson we are to learn from Jesus and the Jews is, that that which is at the bottom of the character of a community is its faith, and that we are therefore to aim to improve it by imparting to it the force and energy of religion. It is not by its policy that a people advances; it is by its faith. That spring of all great endeavor, that secret, inmost spring of all good endeavor of whatever kind, that spring where are the head-waters of all principle, of all morals, of all mutual respect, and all rights, — the faith of a people, its religion, its constant motives, its great rule of conduct, its supreme law, its ultimate standard, its great belief, its hope in death, its undying trust, — this is the fountain which we are to guard, and clear, and deepen, and lay with the smooth, white stones of good institutions, in order that the public character may be pure and wholesome. For where the faith of a people slackens, the character of a people declines; and where it is polluted, the character becomes corrupt; and where it dries up, the public character is dead. Therefore it is, that the institutions of religion are to be jealously guarded, and its appointed days be kept sacred to its uses, and the truth be perpetually preached. And

when, instead of truth, we find practical error proclaimed by ministers of religion, and accepted by the people as holy food, and the servant of God dispenses to a congregation their prejudices, instead of the great verities which control and correct them, it is a dangerous symptom, and the public body is sick. But when we see that it is singly from that one fountain of its faith that the weal of a community can at all flow, how can we be grateful enough to those men, who, though not bound to it by their office, labor to disseminate by church instrumentalities, and on familiar occasions, and by means which public spirit, blessed charity, invents, the truths of the uncorrupted glad tidings of salvation?

You will remember, that this was the way that not only Christ, but the Apostles, labored. Into whatever place they went, they had but one object, to reinvigorate the faith. And this is the work that the Gospel has everywhere done.

3. But many men are not able to exercise any large influence in this respect. A righteous example is always much. But they would hold it presumptuous to attempt to improve men in their religion. There are, then, some of those *applications* of religion, which are commonly called *practical*, because they are immediate, in which all men can act. All men can labor to add to the stock of *honesty* in the community. All men can guard the public *peace*. All men can labor after *truth and simplicity of manners* in their walk and circle. And in doing so, they, under the impulse of the common faith, are tilling some of the chief fruits and productions of it. So, there-

fore, my third reflection is, that we are to aim at the good of the community not by this direct labor in the concerns of its faith *alone.* We occupy a position less central, less *radical*, than that of Christ and the Apostles. They were planting; but we are watering. Much of our labor is rightly confined to the surface. We would not disturb the roots of such a plant as that which God has planted. We add to its fruitfulness and strength by comparatively superficial tillage. General instruction, social urbanity, alms-giving, the public peace, and maintaining of law, are the means by which it is the will of God that we should enter into the Apostles' labors, and by light service reap the fruit of mighty endeavors. And all these things acquire a dignity under Christianity, which they could not have under a heathen dispensation, inasmuch as they are means to the growth of that plant of God, on which all do feed. It is in fact a clearing of the fountain of the public weal, or if not of the fountain, of the channel of the stream in the lower parts of its course. And it is only, my friends, and fellow-citizens, and fellow-Christians, by perpetual vigilance, and the most untiring labor, under the generous impulses of public spirit, that we can secure those blessings which our devout fathers fondly hoped we should enjoy, but which the inroads of the marauding spirit of ungodliness may snatch from us before we have sat down to taste them.

Never, I trust, shall we be called to weep, like Jesus, at foresight of one of those great national wrecks, which form epochs on the rolling tide of time. But many a deep sigh may we bring from our wounded and desponding hearts, as we see the hope of society frustrated, or the form and comeliness of our civic mother stained and marred by sin. But let every Christian be up and doing; that he may earn the right to mourn, if mourn he must, by strenuous exertions for the good and safety of the whole united community.

SERMON II.

MOBS.

I HOPE to be listened to, in what I shall now have to say, with unusual candor. My studies were broken in upon by the note of riot; and my mind has been tossed, through the entire week, with solicitude, lest I should fail, on one side or the other, of my duty. On the one side, I would not be a coward; and on the other, I would not be an intruder. It is well known that I have a degree of sympathy with the Abolitionists. But I do not know that that is a crime. In another place it *was* so considered, by the multitude who only heard of it abroad. But here, I trust, it is not reckoned a crime to share the opinions of Channing, of Franklin, and of Wilberforce.

In my remarks now, I wish not to be thought to insinuate any thing which I do not say. Nothing can be farther from my intention, than to charge any of you with taking part in the late affair. But I fear that some of us were incautiously betrayed into acts and speeches, which tended to increase the excitement. Such a thing is not to be confounded with intentional breach of the peace. I myself, on the other hand, might, in advocating the rights of the fugitive to liberty, unthinkingly let fall words which would tend to encourage a mob to free him. But I should consider myself hardly dealt with, to be charged with the guilt of insurrectionary conduct.

I understand that the fountain of bitterness at this time was not in the bosom of the Church; that, though our friends of the Antislavery cause are apt to pour forth on the Church the vials of their indignation, and sometimes to call its servants any thing but righteous prophets, it was not from the sanctuary, or those who love it, that the disturbance of the peace proceeded. If there were members of this Church compromised, I would not defend them. But I neither insinuate, nor do I believe, that such was the case. And I speak the more cheerfully and freely, because I expect to receive the assent of you all, in nearly every word that I shall say. My object is, together with you, to unfold this business until we see into its true nature. With that view, I have taken for a text the 34th verse of that chapter of the Acts from which I have read to you the portion which most concerns us.

And when they knew that he was a Jew, all with one voice, for about the space of two hours, cried out, "Great is Diana of the Ephesians!" — Acts xix. 34.

This was under the auspices of the heathen goddess. With the progress of Christianity, the art of riot has become more refined. The spread of the Gospel has made plebeian uproars less frequent, but worse. The invention of printing, by extending intelligence, made the people less liable to tumultuous outbreaks, but supplied a means by which their passions could be appealed to with art and effect. The most fatal mobs, therefore, have taken place in recent times and in improved communities. When you add to popular fury the determination of intelligence, and direct this with the sagacity of those who are artists in dissension, you have something which heathen times could not produce, a Christian mob. And the recent specimen we have had of this, though so boyish as to be worthy only of ridicule, was yet so gross in its injuries, — being insulting without being terrible, — and has brought such discredit on us, that it is worthy of being seriously treated. And I propose, in my office of teacher of duty and censor of morals, to which I was ordained in this place, something more than three years since, to attempt to contribute a very little towards setting it in its true light.

It is a little remarkable, that all the mobs of which we read in the New Testament, and of which Christ and his messengers were the objects, were, unless you reckon the occasions on which the Jews were enraged to tumult by Christ's claims of Messianic dignity, all produced by the two causes of irritation which produced the disquiet here, jealousy of foreigners, and apprehension of damage from a suggested reform in the national institutions.

Thus, when Jesus went into the synagogue at Nazareth, which was his own native city, the riot, and attempt to throw him from the precipice on which the city stood, did not arise from his reading the prophecy concerning preaching the Gospel to the poor and deliverance to the captives, and afterward declaring that that day the prophecy was fulfilled in their ears, inasmuch as he was preaching the Gospel to them. They were charmed by his gracious discourse. But when by allusion to Naaman, the Syrian, and the widow at Sarepta, he insinuated, and more than insinuated, that the blessings of Heaven might also, in later times, descend more copiously on Gentiles than on them, as history has proved was indeed the fact, their jealousy of foreigners, and what they considered an insult to their national pride, made them so outrageous, that the person of their teacher was only saved by an apparent miracle.

But in the case before us of Paul at Ephesus, the first excitement arose from a suggestion of a reform in national institutions; not, however, in the way of invasion from abroad, but of persuading the people themselves of a better way. Paul preached to people of his own nation, and to Greeks who had invited him, in the synagogue of the Hebrews, and in the school-house of one Tyrannus, the faith of Christ.

And so soon as that faith was received with favor and produced an effect, the adherents of the ancient system raised a tumult, and called the people together with some appearance of a deliberative assembly, — confused, however, and objectless; and they maintained some appearance of decency, until one Alexander was put forward among them; and when they learned that he was a Jew, a foreigner, they fell to roaring, "Great is Diana of the Ephesians!" and this for the space of some two hours; and it required all the wisdom of a very sensible and calm counsellor to quiet them. But you have seen that we have greatly improved on this example, and that our tumults do not end with vociferation. And it is probable that theirs would not have so ended, if they had not feared to be "called to account" for that day's business. But we have no Romans of whom our people are to be afraid; and having liberty, we know not better than to convert it into license. If Demetrius had a cause of complaint against the man, the law was open, and there were deputies, an abundance of lawyers to undertake the cause. Why did he not bring an action? The fame of the city was known. The institutions were, as the fact proved, safe. The men were neither robbers of churches, nor blasphemers of their religion. They preached, indeed, what they thought was reform in Faith; but they did not compel any to hear, and they did it privately and decently. The tumult, therefore, was absurd and mischievous; but not half so absurd and mischievous as that which we have gone through. Let it not be said or imagined that I have compared our recent visitors with the Apostles. Far from it. But they are probably the only characters in the affair which are not well represented in the scene at Ephesus. There was one, and probably more than one, among us, who, with the good sense of the town clerk of Ephesus, and with all his urbanity, with the knowledge of law, and the dignity of years, resisted this, as he would resist any tumult, for love of the town which is dear to him, and of which he is one of the brightest ornaments. And I venture to say that all who love the Church were on one side in this question, and that those who, under pretence of danger to the Church, raised the excitement, are not the men who, by their piety, have the right to take the Church under their protection; and that those men who, under pretence of love of country, helped in it, are not the men of whom the country would be proud.

First, we strictly deduce from the text, that the fact that a popular riot is excited or threatened is no evidence that the man or cause against which it is excited is in the slightest degree unjust or blamable. For the elements of which a mob is composed are so irrational, and the contagion of a common passion so easily passes from breast to breast,—and the greater part often know not wherefore they are come together,—and the whole proceedings are in general so brutish and violent, that it is not to be regarded as an *expression of opinion* even on the part of those who compose it, but is a mad and blind affair, in which the last appeal is made from reason to passion, from the calm judgments of men to their ignorant prejudices, from the enlightened and the conscientious to the blindest and most abandoned class. A mob, therefore, has nothing of the dignity of an expression of opinion; for it very often has no opinions; and if it have any, they are as discordant as the noises and shouts they make. And it has not the effect of an expression of the people; for we know that a few artful and designing men in the dark, by using all the bad materials they can collect from the purlieus of a large town, can make the show of a great multitude in behalf of a cause which every man who dares exhibit himself disdains.

Law is, indeed, an imperfect protection; for we know that injustice is sometimes perpetrated under its forms. But it is a great shelter; and more than all among *us*, where government, especially *local* government, is weak, and in unusual emergencies cannot be relied on to protect us, it is of the utmost importance that public opinion should be so schooled and trained in justice, as to require that all who will invade other men's privileges, and abridge their rights, attack their persons, and endanger their liberty, should do it by the processes of law; and that when the weak are made an object of attack and violent outrage, the whole community should feel itself insulted, and the more so in proportion to the defencelessness of the sufferers.

In this quiet and hitherto somewhat respectable part of the country, where the thrift and active intelligence of a large town is still combined with remains of village simplicity, and interspersed with something of the amenities of rural life, we are happily ignorant of what a thoroughly excited mob is.

But when at last, and appearances indicate that it will not be long, such a thing is seen, you will learn a most surprising and startling lesson. Quiet people will see forces and terrors aroused, of which they never dreamed as inhabiting the breasts of men, and this town will have read quite a new chapter in the history of humanity. It is a thing wholly unlike any other form of human life, unless it be battle, of which it has the ferocity without the method. A mob is like a wild animal broken from its lair, and is hardly more guided by any principle of reason. The contagion of blind feelings, and the very peculiar excitability of an acting multitude, and the bad passions that take that opportunity to vent themselves, and the malice which then has free play, and, hardly less, the mistaken enthusiasm which imagines something which is not there, and does the more mischief for its honesty, all swelled by idleness and dissipation, combine to make of a multitude of men a *thing*, under the guidance of no soul, having even no intelligent instincts, monstrous in its form, and ferocious in its purposes, a wild and awful force, before which authority and right fall and are trampled in the dust. To enjoy this spectacle in its full sublimity, you need a large, ignorant pauper populace; and for want of this we have been hitherto free from such outbreaks as have shaken Liverpool, and London, and Philadelphia. But our population is rapidly increasing, and since it increases from foreign sources, a part of the increase will be of the uninstructed. We shall acquire more and more the character and habits of a city; and then the science, of which the people are now learning the rudiments, will be fully mastered. Our corporate character is as distinct a thing as the character of an individual. We are now training and forming it, fixing those habits which are to characterize our community fifty years to come, fastening on the town those civic vices and virtues under which our children and successors will thrive or suffer. The character of the town when it becomes a multitudinous city will be, in a measure, what we make it now. The time will come when there will not want materials for a mob of the most destructive character. And even now, by considerable fostering, by those means and appliances which demagogues and bad men know how to use, it is not impossible to excite such a riot, as, if it do not endanger life, threatens property; and, when it cannot terrify the town, is content with disgracing it. Let them go on, it is a good beginning. Let them study this noble, this beneficent art. Let them go to our great cities, and dive into the dark alleys, and consult with mob-captains on the noble art of rioting. Let them have at their command all the unearthly noises to drown the voice of reason, and learn in every place from the most skilful incendiaries how they can most effectively calumniate, and spread abroad in the dark the words which exasperate. They will earn a great reward from their country. The town should turn out to do them honor. It should light up their return with tar-barrels, and commit to their hands the guardianship of the public safety. They must come back with fresh enjoyment to the reading of the Scriptures, and will find instruction for them in the very text which is now before us.

In those vulgar disorders which we have seen, there is this farther to be lamented, that our young men, attracted at first by mere curiosity, take part in them, and there learn the first lessons of plebeian indecency. All who reflect on the important part which the social order has in training the young mind in all the virtues, will know how to regret the circumstance, when he sees our sons joining in these humiliating exhibitions, drinking vulgarity and lawlessness from one fountain, and coming no sooner into the enjoyment of their liberty than they learn to abuse it. We shall not have ourselves to praise, if they do not grow up with habits corresponding to the beginning, — if they do not in time insult their own fathers, and learn with rapidity all the vices, to which the chief barriers are thrown down when they have lost the modesty and subordination which belong to their age.

It is a plain proposition, that every one of us has a right to hear whom he pleases, — under guidance of his conscience and responsible to God, — and that any number of our citizens can claim to assemble and be allowed to discuss any questions of public interest without molestation. And any one who by riotous proceedings interferes with these rights is a traitor to the people, and a public enemy. Such conduct is always a great civil offence, and its enormity is increased when the cause of those who are assailed is just.

In *any* case such proceedings are criminal and alarming; but how peculiarly so, when, as here, the cause was one, certainly of conscience, and, *I* am inclined to think, of philanthropy, and the men worthy of respect. After these insults offered to a stranger, a seeming gentleman, a reputed Christian, every one of us enjoys his liberty of speech only by sufferance, and is liable, whenever he shall become obnoxious to the populace, to be mobbed and hooted through the streets, and his house attacked.

There are moderate men, whose opinions are worthy of all consideration, who think that harm would come of the discussions proposed to be held, that the addresses of the gentlemen would have a tendency to produce insubordination to the laws and disrespect for the government. But even suppose it were so, would you vindicate the honor of the laws by yourself violating them? Would you add fuel to the popular fire on account of your problematical fear, and deny men their commonest rights, to stifle a few arguments? Two ways were open, either to meet what was said and refute it, or neglect it altogether. There was no third. In denying those strangers their right, we, the citizens of Springfield, need not think that they were the chief sufferers; we ourselves have a hundredfold more to bear than they. We have gone down a step in character, and all our rights are compromised in theirs. Public order is the interest of the town, not of the stranger; and freedom of speech is that great right of the people, which cannot in any place be abridged without the liberties of all being thereby endangered. Many feel, and all ought to feel, not only ashamed, but insulted, by the late proceedings. All should feel deeply mortified at the weakness of our government, and interest themselves to make it stronger and more resolute. We ought to have extinguished the flame before it rose. There is little question that it might then have easily been done. Those who have influence, when they saw what was about to happen, ought to have called their friends together and said, " *This must not be* "; they ought to have gone to the selectmen and offered them their service; they ought to have suppressed the note of alarm, discovered, if possible, the secret workers of trouble, and arrested their proceedings. They ought to have said to one another, " Every thing depends on right being now vindicated; we will maintain the law; we are attached to free speech and are determined to defend it, as well when other men speak their minds, as when we speak our own." That would have been the way of faithful public spirit; and we might so have saved our character.

But what a sad, what a pitiful spectacle it was! What a mixture of the vulgar, the nonsensical, and the profane! To begin with those burlesque figures with which some hopeful citizens saw fit to desecrate* the Sabbath, to the scandal of the gathering congregations, that they might insult a stranger, and make Springfield a laughing-stock. For the rope that suspended them was round the neck of all of us, and we are still dangling in ridicule before the whole country. Next, to proceed, with open libel and anonymous calumny, to assail the reputation of one who at least was not a felon, and to gather together a rabble of boys and men to load the air with the

---

* In delivery this was *ornament*.

smoke and stench of their vulgar illumination, and thus, forsooth, honor the cause of government, and vindicate the country against an alien! Are these the things which honor our community? And is this the way in which our better principles are to be maintained against those who, we imagine, wish to invade them?

I suppose from the nature of these things, and from their open advocates, that they are to be considered an example of that attachment to law and order which we recently heard so much vaunted. Would that those pretences had been true! Would that those who profess such attachment to law were attached to it in some other instances than those in which it is oppressive! Would that they could love law in those numerous cases in which it is combined with justice, as well as in an unhappy provision in which it is opposed to it! But no, there are some of our citizens who are zealous for the law only when the law is wrong; and are only then excited to enthusiasm, when, by happy accident, they can, by obeying the magistrate, violate conscience. All their souls are fired in behalf of a statute to which humanity is sacrificed. When only justice is to be maintained, and mere right to be vindicated, and men to be protected in their legal and just privileges, their zeal for law and order subsides, and lies very low.

It is my duty to remind you that the guilt of a riot lies chiefly on those who intentionally instigate it. For half-bred and half-educated men and boys will often join in mobs from mere idleness, or curiosity, or misapprehension; but the intelligent man who uses these materials as his tools employs men's brutish passions to overawe reason and truth, — he is the traitor and the greater culprit. Said Jesus to that wretched tool, Pontius Pilate, "Thou couldst have no power at all against me except it were given thee from above; therefore, he that delivered me unto thee hath the greater sin."

I put to the whole town these questions: —

Whether a man's reputation is less his own, or we less culpable for injuriously assailing it, because he was born in England, and we bound to him by the duties of hospitality?

Whether it has generally been found more serviceable to truth to stifle discussion, or to let it have free course?

Whether any one of us would have suffered such treatment in any town of England in consequence of any exercise of his free speech, and whether, if the populace had so annoyed him, he would not have found prompt protection from the public authorities?

I am myself, as a citizen of Springfield and pastor of one of her churches, inexpressibly mortified and ashamed at our people's unwashed, dissolute behavior; and I consider my own rights to have been seriously invaded; and there are very many — I trust all of you — think with me.

A mob, my friends, may always be considered as lying dormant in the hiding-places of a large town's depravity. It is sometimes a dangerous, many-headed monster, and sometimes only a venomous reptile. When it next creeps forth upon us, and stimulated by its natural food, libel and liquor, displays itself in our streets in open riot, I trust it will be scourged back to its holes with the threefold lash of truth, justice, and the penal law.

It remains to be seen, whether a dozen mistaken and violent men are to hazard the peace, and defy the rights of every one of us.

We read that, on an awful occasion, the Saviour of the world was brought and exhibited to the people bleeding from the scourge. That which was guilt and horror then might be justice and leniency now, if the scourge were only the scourge of public reprobation.

If good counsels could prevail, I would have all who took lead in these transactions brought up, with constables staves in their hands, and ranged side by side upon the platform of that hall, and all the people admitted to look at them, and identify them. And in large letters on a scroll over their heads I would have this inscription:— GEORGE WASHINGTON DESERVED WELL OF THE NATION; BUT THESE MEN HAVE SERVED THEIR COUNTRY ACCORDING TO THEIR CONSCIENCES. And as the sword is made to figure in statues of noble men, I would have all their various weapons and implements, their filthy missiles, their tar, and their feathers, and their characteristic materials, laid in open sight on the platform with them. That moral pillory should be their punishment.

If the citizens would be guided by my advice, they would let any man who visited us enjoy all his legal rights, and regard any one who molested him in them as their own enemy, and make him feel in its utmost extent the rigor of the law. They would feel in the abridgment of others' rights themselves attacked, and the public safety seriously endangered. They would appoint an officer to attend meetings which it was apprehended would be indecent, corrupting to the public morals, or blasphemous towards religion and the Church, and cause instant prosecution to be made for the offence. They would appoint a committee to attend where it was supposed the character of citizens would be attacked, and cause the offender to be prosecuted for detraction and slander. Thus every stranger should feel, not only the just protection, but the just restraints, of the law; he should see the shield and the sword of the law both at his side; and they should be instruments sacred as an altar, and impartial as Rhadamanthus. But we shall have nothing more to boast of our country, when we forget justice and abuse liberty.

It has been attempted to palliate the business by comparing it to other riots which some consider half defensible. The mob at Boston was a violent overriding of the law; and executive officers ought to be armed with such force as entirely to preclude its repetition. But that was made by ignorant blacks, whom the (national) Constitution, (as it is administered, practically) disfranchises, and who consequently were not bound by the peculiar obligations of citizenship (to the extent that we are); ours was by men enjoying unimpaired all the privileges of citizens. The object of that was to restore a man to his natural rights; the object of this was to invade rights, and deprive a man of privileges which all the laws secure. That was to secure liberty, and this was to destroy it. The spirit of that was generosity, the spirit of this was malice. That was at least courageous and by open day, this was cowardly and skulked into the darkness of the night.

A still more flagitious attempt is made to confound this with that reluctant and peaceable refusal to obey the law, which some have thought might in certain circumstances be their duty. But, whatever men may pretend, they know full well that the two things cannot be confounded. One who shall see no difference between the refusal of Daniel to fall down before Nebuchadnezzar's image, the refusal of the Apostles to obey the senate of the Jews, the refusal of an American to help in binding a slave, or to help in starving him, — between this and the proceedings with which we have been favored this week, — is incapable of discerning the rules of human conduct.

If a strong man had in open day taken the stranger by the collar in the street, and told him that, if he opened his mouth in town, he would cudgel him, it would have been a ruffian outrage, but would have had the merit of honesty and boldness. But to league together in numbers, and do that impersonally and in the dark which will not bear the day, is not an example of the civic virtues which in *any* time would have adorned and saved the state.

It is highly probable, that, when the generation of night-disturbers is in its grave, a generation of daylight ruffians will come, and that in party times — to say nothing of the tender sex — even a *man* will have to walk the streets with caution. It may be that self-styled committees of vigilance will be appointed to interrogate and regulate us. But I trust that then, should, by some singular change in the public spirit, all other places fall under the interdict of our guardians, truth and freedom will find refuge in the Christian pulpit. I trust it will be long ere men will lay their insolent hands on that, and attempt to enslave that which our *religion* has made free. And when the people address the ministry, which is their handmaid in virtue, and, dreaming that she is a captive, say to her, " Sing us one of the pleasant songs of Zion," I hope the reply will be, " Nay, I will declare the truth of the Lord, which shall be sweeter than songs in the ears of the righteous."

THE END.

www.ingramcontent.com/pod-product-compliance
Lightning Source LLC
LaVergne TN
LVHW011133110826
845150LV00008B/2313

* 9 7 8 1 4 1 8 1 9 3 8 7 4 *